Coloring Through the Year

The Coloring Cafe

by Ronnie Walter

Book layout, illustrations and photographs © Ronnie Walter

Coloring Through the Year-The Coloring Cafe/Ronnie Walter
ISBN: 978-1-956772-07-4

Welcome to The Coloring Café®!

Hello, Friend!

Welcome to the Coloring Cafe! This book contains 35 pages to color—color I order or skip around to celebrate your favorite times of the year!

I recommend using fine tipped markers, colored pencils, watercolor pencils or pan watercolors. All can be found at any local craft store or online. A heavy application of paint can make the paper buckle a bit so I would use a light hand when using water based paints. Some of the details could be difficult to capture with crayons, but you can certainly use them if you prefer. If you use markers, slip a scrap piece of heavier paper (like card stock) between the pages in case of bleed-through.

Remember, coloring should be relaxing—and that includes relaxing your expectation for perfection. My drawings are quirky and certainly not perfect, but I love making them for you! My intention is to provide you an opportunity to find a calm and pleasant moment in your day. So enjoy!

Thank you so much!

TO LODGE

SUNSHINE

UMBRELLAS

SPRING THINGS

fresh grass

GREEN LEAVES

flowers

HAPPY EASTER

More books from The Coloring Café!

Christmas in Your Heart Coloring Book
The Coloring Cafe-Volume One
The Coloring Cafe-Volume Two
The Coloring Cafe-To Go!
The Coloring Cafe-Inspired Heart
The Coloring Cafe-Bible Blessings to Color
The Coloring Café-Stress Relief
The Coloring Café-Fashion Girls
The Coloring Café-Paper Dolls to Color
The Coloring Cafe-Colorful Christmas
The Coloring Cafe-Christmas in Your Heart

The Coloring Cafe-Happy Times
The Coloring Cafe-You've Got This, Girl!
The Coloring Cafe-Everyday Angels
The Coloring Cafe-Affirmations
The Coloring Cafe-You Are Enough
Easy & Simple Everyday Large Print Coloring Book
Easy & Simple Mandalas Large Print Coloring Book
Easy & Simple Bible Verse Large Print Coloring Book
Easy & Simple Christmas Large Print Coloring Book
Cuppa Calm-An Inspirational Coloring Journal
Cuppa Cute-A Fashion Inspired Coloring Journal

Books for KIDS from The Coloring Café!

The Coloring Cafe-Colorful KIDS-AMAZING ME!
The Coloring Cafe-Colorful KIDS at Christmas
The Coloring Cafe-Happy Kids Color Christmas
The Coloring Cafe-Happy Kids Color Animals
The Coloring Cafe-Happy Kids Color Their World
The Coloring Cafe-Happy Kids Color Monsters
The Coloring Cafe-The Big Fun Coloring Book for Toddlers

From CQ Publishing:

The Coloring Café-It's a Girl Thing
The Coloring Café-My Cup Runneth Over
The Coloring Café-Happy Everything
The Coloring Café- Kindness Matters
The Coloring Café-Relax, Unwind and Color

The Coloring Café-Life is Delicious
The Colorful Café-Colorful Blessings
The Coloring Cafe-Home is Where it All Begins
The Coloring Café-Be the Sunshine

About The Artist

Ronnie Walter is an artist and award winning writer. She licenses her illustrations on all kinds of products including stickers, greeting cards, stationery, giftware, fabric and more.

Besides the creator of the popular Coloring Cafe series of coloring books, Ronnie is the author of **Bernice-The Cow Who Loved Christmas**, **License to Draw! How to Monetize your Art through Art Licensing...and more!** and **Gruesome Greetings, A Georgie Hardtman Mystery.**

Ronnie lives in a little house by the water with her husband Jim Marcotte and the best shelter dog ever, Larry.

Email: coloringcafe@gmail.com
Facebook: Coloring Cafe
Instagram: @thecoloringcafe #thecoloringcafe
Twitter: @thecoloringcafe

www.thecoloringcafe.com

Made in the USA
Coppell, TX
25 February 2023